Portuguese Water Dogs as Pets

A Complete 'Portie' Owner's Guide

Portie Dogs General Info, Purchasing, Care, Cost, Diet, Health, Supplies, Grooming, Training and More Included!

By: Lolly Brown

Foreword

United States President Barack Obama and his family put a spotlight on the Portuguese Water Dog breed when they decided to keep one as a pet in the country's presidential residence - the White House. From the name itself, this breed loves to swim in the water and play around the beach with their owners especially with children. Also known as the 'Portie,' this rare water – loving canine is a kind of pet that prefers to be wet and loves to soak in bodies of water and enjoys the rain more than any other dog breed which is why it's very important to consider this one important factor before fully committing to keeping one as a household pet. Caveats aside, the Portuguese Water Dog is a curly mop of good natured dog breed that might be the right pet for you and your family.

The Portie needs lots of exercise not to mention your love and attention. They can happily live in an apartment, a large country estate, a small suburban home or in the case of former President Obama's residence – a historical site. Porties must be supervised especially if you're going to let him/ her play around in your backyard as they wouldn't like to be alone and prefer your company.

This book will guide you on how you to properly care for your pet Portuguese water dog. You'll get to learn more about the Portie's history, biological information, training and grooming needs, health, and the proper diet to keep your pet healthy and happy! Always keep in mind to treat your portie water dog as if he/she is not just an outdoor pet but a part of your family.

Table of Contents

Introduction

The Portuguese Water Dog is a medium – sized breed that's also strong, robust, and also possess great endurance and stamina. They are classified as a working dog and had been beneficial for many years. As a household pet, the dog is not just energetic but also smart, loving, and loyal. They are perfect as a family companion, and can also serve as a guard dog. However, just like any other pets, they will demand your full attention and should always be supervised especially if they are hanging out outside. This is the kind of pet that easily bonds with family, and a very loyal mate to their owners. Porties also get along very well with other household pets but can even get a bit competitive for attention; they will try to be as humorous as they can just to be in the center stage. As a guard dog, this breed is protective to its owners but not in an aggressive way. They are alert and quite cautious especially when it comes to strangers.

The playful nature and fluffy – looking appearance usually belies its true character as a hardworking, independent and tough dog which is why it may not be a suitable pet for everyone. Its personality is quite complex but just like all household pets, they just wanted to be trusted and love by people around them.

The Portuguese Water Dog can live anywhere between 12 and 15 years. They usually tend to slowly mature, and they are still pretty active even if they already reached their senior years. In line with this, daily exercise outdoors is required otherwise your portie will find a way to provide its own form of exercise indoors – which might involve running around the house and all over your furniture. These dogs require an active lifestyle, and they also need to be mentally stimulated. They are the type of breed that loves to be involved in your everyday business so make sure to always keep them at bay in your daily affairs.

The Portuguese Water Dog will surely enjoy a structured activity in order to channel their cleverness and high level of energy. You may want to get them involved in obedience and agility activities such as water work, Rally – O games or flyball as all of these will make your pet bond with your/ your family and also enable to thrive and channel out their limitless energy.

It's very rare if your Portuguese water dog breed doesn't prefer to be in the water. They love to splash around and get wet which is why you need to make sure that you provide your pet with access to water especially in areas that aren't near swimming pools, beaches, rivers, lakes, or other bodies of water.

The Portie is not like any other kennel dogs; it loves to socialize with people in general, and get along with other pets quite well as long as there is proper introduction. You need to interact with them on a daily basis so that they can develop a great personality in the long run.

The dog breed has been used as a working dog by Portuguese fishermen back in the day. The fishermen used to bring them to the Grand Banks cod fishery which is located off the coast of Newfoundland, and frankly quite far from their homeland. These dogs are like coastal retrievers in Portugal for many centuries. The Porties were vital 'crew members' as they help fishermen pull in the nets and deliver the fishes between boats. It is believed that the portie and the poodle dog breed have a common ancestor. The may have helped in developing the Irish Water Spaniel dog breed.

The Portuguese Water Dog's importance in the fishing industry have declined over the years and they eventually became a rare dog breed. In 1958, the first members of the Portie breed reached United States.

However, it wasn't until 1972 that the breed became known to American and an organization called Portuguese Water Dog Club of America was officially formed. In 1984, the Portuguese Water Dog was officially recognized by the American Kennel Club (AKC). In recent years, the Portie ranked around 55th to 60th in the registered dog breeds by the AKC. The breed became very popular when it became part of the First Family President Barack Obama – a first in the history of the breed

Chapter One: All About the 'Portie'

The Portuguese Water Dog was developed in Portugal, and thanks to the fishermen, this particular dog breed had gotten used to being around bodies of water and became quite fond of getting wet. This is because they served as the fisherman's right hand man for centuries during their fishing endeavors. Needless to say, these cute and fluffy dogs were once part of the 'crew' – they used to help their mates retrieved nets, carry around fish bags from one boat to another, deliver messages, serve their masters, and pretty much do anything that their owners tasked them to do with finesse and enthusiasm.

As time goes by, fewer people need the breed's water – logged service which is why the Portuguese Water Dog's cleverness and obedience have been put to other uses. They were used to retrieve home run balls that went to the water during baseball games particularly at the time when San Francisco opened its new bayside ballpark for the San Francisco Giants. A group of Porties became known as the Baseball Aquatic Retrieval Korps (BARK), and eventually became quite an attraction of their own.

As you many now have learned, the portie will happily do almost anything you asked of them if you choose to keep them as a pet. The breed's hard – working, obedient and loyal character also serves them well in many canine sports as well as various outdoor activities like hiking, boating, and helping children chase a soccer ball – or any ball for that matter. You won't have problems for creating activities for your pet Portie but you'll surely have a problem keeping up with their energy. You need to find the time to make sure that your pet is busy and well – cared for. It's not ideal that you acquire this breed if you or your family doesn't have time to spare because they need your full attention.

This breed is a great family pet and they are usually great with children but they will need to be supervised especially if they child is too young. The Portuguese Water Dog can be quite rambunctious at times and some Porties are quite large and heavy which can be too much for toddlers to handle.

This chapter will provide you with information regarding the Portuguese Water Dog's amazing personality and temperament. You'll also get to learn the pros and cons of keeping one as a pet.

Facts and Quirks

- This dog breed sports a curly to wavy coat that comes in a variety of colors with or without white markings. The most common coat colors are black and brown. The least common color is a white coated portie.

- The Portie breed can also remain fully coated or sport a sort of 'lion' clip with a bare rear. Their coat can be wavy or curly.

- Portuguese water dog breeds that sports a curly coat are somewhat more loosely coiled than that of a Poodle dog breed. They also don't shed as much but if left untrimmed, obviously they will continue to grow and can be quite a chore for you so make sure that you keep up with their grooming needs. We will discuss more about grooming in the next few chapters.

- This may not be the right pet for people with allergies although some may be able to tolerate them. However, keep in mind that there's no such thing as a dog that will not cause any sort of allergic reaction. What you can do if you're quite sensitive is to make sure to get your portie groomed every other month and brush their coats thoroughly at least every week.

Temperament and Personality

Portuguese water dogs have three qualities that make them stood out of the rest of the dog breeds: cleverness, obedience, and energy. It's a very agile dog breed that thrives for physical and mental stimulation. Needless to say, the more challenging something is for them, the more they enjoy doing it. Apart from these great traits, they are also a family – friendly dog that loves to look after their owners because they treat their owners as "part of the pack." These pets need to be with a family because they don't like being left alone at home or left for a long period of times in their kennels. This dog breed thrives in the midst of an active family.

The Portuguese water dog highly requires vigorous exercise activities that will enable them to sharpen their agility and obedience skills. It's ideal that you prepare activities like canine sports, daily romps and of course swimming! Due to its heritage as a water dog, this breed has a special affinity for water – related activities, making swimming the best way for them to burn off their energy and have fun at the same time.

This dog breed is also a natural when it comes to playing with kids. However, the dog's natural exuberance may cause them to play a bit rough with children so make sure that an adult is supervising them or you have taught/ trained your pet to play nicely with people and keep his mouth to himself. It's also best to teach your kids to not make any rough plays with the dog to avoid any sort of mishaps.

Training and Socialization

Just like any other dog breeds, the portie pup should preferably be trained at a young age. Even if these dogs are just 8 weeks old, they can already learn some good manners. It's best to train and socialize them before they reach 6 months old. We also highly recommend that you enroll your portie pup in a puppy kindergarten class if possible when he/she reaches between 10 and 12 weeks old because this is the best age to teach them basic training and socialization skills. However, you should also be aware that many puppy training classes require the pups to be vaccinated with kennel cough or the likes; it must also be up – to – date. There are also many vets that recommend the young pups to have limited exposure to public places and other dogs until they receive the needed vaccinations such distemper, parvovirus, and rabies and that these vaccines have been completed.

In line with the formal dog training, you can already start your pups with the basics and already socialize them among friends and family while you're waiting for the vaccines to be completed. Once you already received a go – signal from your vet, then you're good to enroll them to a training class. Such training and socialization experiences will help the young pup grow as an obedient, sensible, and well – mannered adult dog.

It's best to talk to an experienced and reputable portie breeder so that you'll exactly know the kind of canine companion you're looking for, and how you can select the best pup. Breeders are the ones who interact daily with their pups making them the best person to ask for recommendations regarding the personality and temperament of the pups available for sale. We will give you tips on how you can select the best portie pup and determine a reputable breeder in the next few chapters.

Porties with Childrens and Pets

Vets and portie breeders highly recommend potential dog owners to take the time to properly socialize the breed so that they can get along well with other potential pets and people. Larger – sized porties may be more suited for older kids than young ones because toddlers may not be able to keep up with the dog's high energy. Portuguese water dog breeds in general will love to play with kids of all ages but some porties may be quite rambunctious than the other so make sure that the personality of the pet you will choose will also suit your kids so that they can handle them well.

If your kids learn to get along with your pet, they can surely have a great time playing with one another and this can be a great exercising opportunity both for your dog and your children. You'll also find that porties are such a ball of energy even if they are already well into their senior years.

Porties also get along with other household pets such as cats or dogs but you need to ensure that they are properly introduced and socialized. It's also ideal that you raise your portie together with your other pets so that they will grew up together and get used to being with each other.

We do not recommend that you get more than one Portie dog because it may be too much to handle for most people especially if it's your first time of owning a pet dog. These dog breed demands attention from their owners and requires daily exercise and mentally stimulating activities which can take up most of your time. However, if you think you can handle keeping two Portuguese water dogs. It's highly recommended that you acquire a male and female, that's both neutered and around one year apart. If they are not neutered or spayed then they will most likely have territoriality issues or even unwanted pregnancies. Make sure to supervise your pet dog with another pet, be it a dog or cat, until you are sure that they're safe to be left with one another or until their relationship is already established.

Your water loving dog would love to enter dog competitions such as athletic events, agility games, fly – dog, and obedience competitions. You can expect them to excel at these kinds of events provided of course that you help them when it comes to training and other athletic or intelligence demands that these competitions require. Some porties get intimidated by large crowds and other animals especially if they're not properly socialized which is why it's best to get them used to interacting with as many people as possible in preparation for the event so that they are comfortable when joining competitions. If you are considering your pet to compete, it's probably best to hire a professional dog trainer so that your dog can maximize its potential. Competitions will be a rewarding experience for both you and y our dog, such events can also form a strong and bonded relationship.

Pros and Cons

The American Kennel Club calls Portuguese water dogs as a self – willed, and courageous dog. It has a great disposition and a breed that's very resistant to fatigue. Emotionally speaking though, this dog is quite sensible and stable despite its energetic and athletic trait. It is poised for any type of activity which is why walking them around the neighborhood or taking them with you for a run is beneficial as it will meet their exercise requirements. And since they are a master when it comes to swimming, make sure to bring them out for a dive or splash in the water as much as possible.

Mental stimulation is just as important as the physical activities. Make sure to let them practice their intelligence over some form of mentally stimulating activities like fetching games, advanced obedience activities, and all sorts of agility sports. If you're not the outdoorsy type of person or you want a lap dog then the Portie breed is definitely not for you.

A well – socialized portie will react to towards strangers differently and may range from friendly to polite. However, this dog is always alert, knows how to hold his ground, and quite steadfast making him a fine guard dog. Most porties are welcoming of other household pets especially if they are raised with them. However, you must still properly introduce them to avoid any conflicts especially if the other pet is a different dog breed. You must know the personality and temperament of your pets so that you'll have an idea on how you're going to introduce them and make them get along even without your supervision. Portuguese Water Dogs are independent, has a great sense of humor, and strong – minded. They are looking for a consistent leader so as a potential portie owner you must show them consistency especially whenever you are training them.

The Portuguese Water Dog is a natural retriever which is why the Portuguese fishermen took notice of this trait. It's quite a mouthy dog who loves to pick up, nibble and chew on everything in his path regardless if the object is edible or not. They will also try to gnaw on your hands.

Make sure to provide a box of chew toys so that your portie can satisfy its chewing urges through carrying something around its mouth. Young porties are also more rambunctious compared to older ones. Pups get bored easily if they're not given attention and structured activities otherwise they will to excavate your backyard or chew on your furniture which can result to long – term behavioral problems.

Pros

- Porties are athletic, agile and a durable medium – sized dog.
- They shed less than other similarly coated breed since their shed hairs are trapped in their wavy or curly coat.
- These dogs love to be outdoors and love to engage in athletic activities.
- They like to play with kids and interact well with the family as well as with strangers.
- They make a great watch dog but they're too polite to be a guardian

- They get along with other household pets provided that they are properly introduced.
- They are not choosy eaters, they are not usually prone to diseases, and they are affectionate, loyal and obedient to their owners.
- They can be easily trained and socialize at a young age.

Cons

- They require vigorous exercise daily
- They are quite jumpy and rowdy especially at a young age
- They can be destructive if they got bored or if they don't properly burn their energy off due to lack of exercise.
- They are independent and strong – willed which means they require a confident owner who can handle them and act as a leader.
- They need to be regularly clipped and brushed
- They are quite the mouthy type of dog breed – they love to chew on everything and gnaw on people's hands.

Chapter Two: Selecting a Portie Breeder and Portie Puppy

This chapter will provide you with tips on how you can select the right portie pup for you as well as the things you need to know when it comes to finding a reputable breeder. You'll also learn the legal side of acquiring a pet portie from contracts to bill of sale, and from health guarantees to registration application. You'll also learn what to expect if you choose to purchase a puppy versus an older and matured Portuguese water dog.

Breeder Finder 101

Ask Your Vet!

One of the first things you need to do is to find a reputable dog breeder. It's best if you buy your pet from breeders who specialize in Portuguese water dog breeding because you can be sure that they can help you out when it comes raising your pet even after they already made a sale. What you can do is to ask your local vet for recommendations on where or who to buy a Portie breed from.

Check Online

You can also check resources online, or ask people from forums to ask them where they bought their puppies from. This will not only save you time and energy in finding the right breeder but you'll also get somewhat of an assurance from past buyers. If the breeder is highly recommended by people around your area or in a particular forum, then chances are that they are responsible and reputable.

Do Your Own Due Diligence

It's very important that you still do your own research or due diligence, and perhaps create a checklist of the qualities you like in a breeder to see if he/she fits your own criteria. It's very important that you not just make a connection with your puppy but also with the one who bred them. You can start off by asking questions to see how well they know their breeds, and also the terms of contract so that you'll be guaranteed of a quality pet. We will talk about this more later in this section. It's also highly recommended that you consider adopting dogs from rescue centers, if in case a Portie is available. It will be less expensive, and you'll also get to save a life.

Purchasing a Portie Pup

Prior to buying a Portie, you need to know whether you should get a pup or a much older Portie. This section will provide you with the pros and cons of purchasing a puppy versus an adult Portie. Taking the time to consider the pros and cons is very important at the onset in order to avoid any problems in the future particularly in terms of general care and budget.

For instance, you may need to consider asking yourself questions such as do you think you have the time to train a puppy? How much time can you set aside for puppy training? Are you patient when it comes to working with young canines? Do you have the budget to meet the needs of the pup? Do you have time to play and interact with them on a daily basis? Make sure to keep these questions in mind before purchasing a pup.

What to Expect from a Portie Pup

Puppies are obviously the cutest and most adorable stage in any dog's life. If you want to soak in their lovable and energetic personalities then consider getting a pup instead of an adult. Young porties will surely bring joy to your life the moment you wake up in the morning. Getting a puppy is best suited for individuals and families who can spend quality time with a young dog. If you plan on raising your Portie according to your standards, and you're focus on properly training them to meet you or your family's want or needs, then you'll have better chances with a pup compared to an adult.

However, you need to spend quality time with your Portuguese water dog puppy and form a bond with them so that they will be easier to train or socialize. Some people get a pup but they are not in the house all the time or they don't take the time to train them, and they wonder why their pets are misbehaving. If you want your portie to become a well – mannered pet as it grows, you must give time and attention to it, and not just provide their basic needs. Choosing to purchase a puppy from a reputable source or adopting one from a rescue shelter will make the dog stay longer as part of your family since it will recognize that you're the one providing them with all their basic needs and general care as they grow.

Prior to buying a puppy from the breeder, it is best that you take the time to see how they interact and play with other dogs as this will give you a hint when it comes to temperament and personality. Usually, puppies that grew in a litter tend to be more assertive and aggressive than puppies that are raised alone which is why the former might be harder to train. The latter though may tend to be more reserved especially with strangers, which is why socialization at an early age is important. Some owners find it difficult to manage and raise a pup especially if they have their own families to take care of. You have to keep in mind that raising a puppy whether it's a Portuguese water dog breed or not is very the most challenging stage.

That being said, you need to ensure that you have the time to let your pup meet new people, other pets, and take them out for a walk around the neighborhood. As puppies grow, you'll soon find out that they also go through the stubborn stage just like a child. If you're sort of a neat freak and you want everything organize around the house, getting a puppy may not be best for you because at some point they can damage your furniture and other household items especially when they go through the chewing stage. As with Portie pups, they are chewer dogs and a bit rambunctious; expect them to be very playful and prepare chew toys for them because they would want to chew/ gnaw everything they see including your hands! You need to puppy – proof your house and also housebreak your pup so that they wouldn't run over everything.

Needless to say, you have to have lots of patience if you plan on getting a pup. If you want training to be effective, you also have to be consistent with your methods and the schedule otherwise as Portie pups require owners who are consistent leaders just like what we've talked about in the previous chapter.

Picking the Pup

When you have already decided on where or who you're going to buy your Portie puppy from, it's time to find which puppy you're going to take home. You can try out the strategies or tips below when deciding which one to get especially if your breeder has quite a handful of litters. One of the techniques that are recommended by some dog experts is to put a ribbon on the puppies that you're going to choose from. This way you can easily identify which is which even if they look identical to one another. It'll also be easy to make mental notes to see which one you prefer.

Check out the tips below:

- **Interact with the pups**

  The breeder will most likely lead you to the play pen where the puppies are, all you have to do is observe how the puppies play with one another. This is where you can see if one is perhaps more active than the other, or how high or low their energy levels are but since you're going to buy a Portie, expect that the pups have high levels in varying degrees.

- **Determine the hyper level of your chosen portie**

  When it comes to choosing hyper breeds such as the Portuguese water dogs though, you also have to keep in mind that it may result in conflict if you are keeping another active dog at home. What you want to have is a puppy that's not shy or someone who is afraid to come to you. You can lean over them and let them sniff your finger, and see how they'll react. You don't want to pick a puppy that's intimidated or aggressive. If the puppies are interactive to you, that's a good sign of having a nice temperament. You'll easily notice their differences, and you can also get up close to them. You may find that one might be gentler than the other, or perhaps more active than the rest. You can also ask the breeder to put in another puppy that is of a different breed so that you can see how the Porties will react and welcome another kind. This can also help you if the puppy of your choice is someone who can get along well with other dog breeds.

- **Put the Portie/s to the Test**

  Once all the puppies get to know you, it's time to put them to the test to see which one best suits you and connect with you on a personal level. The best option is to really acquire your Portie from a breeder that's an expert in this particularly canine. You can find lots of Portie breeder across the country. Although it may cost a bit more expensive compared to buying from pet stores or adopting from rescue shelters, you can be sure of the dog's quality.

What to Expect from an Adult Portie

If you acquire your adult portie from a reputable breeder, the dog will most likely be trained already. You can expect him or her to already know how to behave around the house, on the leash, or whenever you're out for a walk. Training is still a must but it'll be less time consuming since they're already matured compared to training a pup. Same amount of love and care is needed but less emphasis on training concepts. This is the reason why some would – be owners find it more advantageous to acquire an adult Portie because you easily know its overall appearance and size as well as its personality and behavior. And since most adult dogs are socialized, trained and housebroken already which means that it can save you time and skip all the difficult parts of dog keeping.

Most matured Porties will still be as excited as a pup when introduced to a new surrounding which is why it's still best to continue the socialization and housebreaking training once you bring your pet home. An adult portie may take just a few days to adjust to its new environment so just give him time to settle and explore your house.

Perhaps, the biggest disadvantage of buying an adult dog is that it'll be harder to change any of the negative behavior (if any). If you find that your dog adapted a bad habit from its previous owner, it might be very difficult to correct. It's still possible to retrain him but it could be confusing for your pet. You will need to take effort if you want to change a particular habit you don't like and encourage them with treats or use positive reinforcement. Patience is a must if this is going to be your problem.

However, if you find that your adult Portie doesn't listen to you or are showing signs of misbehaving, make sure to take the time to give them positive attention and socialize with them so that they'll develop a good relationship with you. Some adults may find it hard to settle in a new environment and this is where it usually becomes difficult to handle. Adult Portuguese water dogs may also be harder to introduce and/ or socialize with your other household pets, which is why you need to ensure that you monitor them whenever they're interacting with one

another.

When it comes to basic needs, it's almost the same

with puppies. Make sure that your adult dog is getting the

right amount of food, has enough space around the house

where they can have exercising opportunities, and that their

health is taken care of. You will need to make sure that

they're neutered or spayed to avoid any aggressive behavior

or unwanted pregnancies.

Picking the Right Adult Portie

Aside from the basic interaction tests given earlier

when selecting the right portie pup, you need to also

consider other factors when choosing an adult such as the

lineage of the dog, the reputation of the breeder itself, the

color of the coat and also the markings of the dog, and

whether or not they are a champion dog.

Champion Porties

Championship lines of Porties are usually more expensive than non – performance dog breeds. Non – performance Portuguese water dogs cost around $2,500 while puppies from championship lineages may cost anywhere way more than the average price. Keep in mind that there could be additional expense for shipping costs. Most legit breeders already have their pups and adult dogs' micro - chipped prior to purchasing. The health certificates and registration papers and contract are already included in the price of a purebred Portie.

The Legal Side of Acquiring a Portie

Once you have decided that you're going to purchase a portie either a pup or an adult, the next thing to do is to acquire the dog legally. You need to ask your breeder to come up with a contract because it will serve as the bill of sale for your Portie pup. The contract must clearly state the rights that have been agreed upon by you and your breeder. The contract is a binding agreement so make sure that before you sign, you have already asked any concerns you might have before you finalize everything. Here are some of the things included in the contract:

- You need to ask for a bill of sale because this will be your proof of dog ownership. Make sure that you understand the legal aspects before purchasing a puppy or dog. Many places in the U.S. require animals to have a health report to ensure that the puppy is getting the right health vaccinations. If you find that your pet is unhealthy, you can still return it to the breeder within 48 hours. This will depend on your binding agreement with the breeder and what the law will require in your area of residence.

- You need to also ask for the registration application. This is included in the contract and it is usually filled out by the breeder or seller. He/ she needs to fill in the details of the breed such as the sex, color, physical characteristics, date of birth, name of parents, registration numbers, and other health – related info. The breeder will need to include their name or their business' name, and it must be affix with their signature. The seller must provide a lineage statement or attached a copy of the pup's lineage chart. This is very important especially if you bought a championship Portie breed.

- You need to also ensure that there's a health guarantee. The agreement should state that the breeder has ensured that the dog is free from any diseases, both genetic and hereditary conditions, which may not be present at the time of your purchase.

Chapter Three: Shelter and Supplies for Your Porties

Just like us humans, dogs also like the idea of having space and freedom. They also tend to like an open backyard to play in or a property to roam around but at the end of the day, they want some place to den in. Dogs, no matter how active or interactive they are throughout the day, would also like to rest in a preferably close and cozy space. It's the same with cats, birds, spiders, and other creatures – they also want to have some sort of privacy. You also have to understand that whether you buy your pet a crate or not, your Portie is most probably denning up one way or another.

Even if the Portuguese water dog is a very active and sociable dog, you can expect them to cozy up between you or your family on the bed or lounging on their own bed. This is where a crate comes in. It is a soft and protective den that your Portie can use whenever you're not around to be with them. There are some dogs who don't need crates but those are the outliers. Majority of dogs especially puppies will surely benefit from crate training and its useful function. This chapter will provide you information about using crates for your pet Portie as well as the supplies you need to prepare before you acquire them.

All About Crates for Your Portie

Crates are useful especially if you're raising a puppy or aiding a new adult dog to settle in their new environment. While your pet Portie is learning your house rules, using a crate can help you control destructive behaviors. Even for those dogs that don't need a crate, crate training is still essential because it could build up their character as you may need your dog to go to the crate at some point nonetheless. Say for example, they need a place to stay while you're off somewhere or while waiting their turn at the groomers, they will need to spend time inside the crate. It's also a safe option whenever you plan on bringing your Portie while travelling as it can be a familiar and reliable place inside the car for your dog, and you're guaranteed that they won't cause any distraction while you're driving especially since Porties are quite active pets.

Crates will provide management for your Portie. It will somewhat prevent them from getting tempted to chew things by blocking their access to certain things around the house like shoes or clothes. Aside from that crates can be necessary and quite effective when it comes to housetraining a puppy or a matured or adult dog. However, even if that's the case, they still need to do the full housetraining. For mature dogs that already have gone through the potty training process, a crate may not be necessary but if ever your adult pet has behavior issues you're trying to address then a crate can be a useful component to your treatment plan.

Crate Types and Standard Size

The most common suggestion of keepers when it comes to the size of the cage is that the crate should be big enough for the dog to stand up, turn around, and lie down. This suggestion may be useful if you're adopting a more mature Portie but for puppies it might be quite difficult. Wire crates usually come with a small divider so that once your pet starts growing, you can easily adjust and enlarge the cage so that you don't need to keep buying. However, for your plastic crate you may need to buy a crate big enough to accommodate your pet's growth.

Pros and Cons of Using Different Types of Crates

Pros and Cons of Using Plastic Crates:

- Plastic crates are very easy to clean up because you can disassemble it so that you can do a spot – cleaning.
- It's generally warmer and drier. It's also very easy to just throw a blanket on it to create a dark and denned up space for your portie.

- Plastic crates are good for cars or whenever you're travelling with your pet, some crates can also be easily strapped to the car seat.
- Plastic crates are also the only option whenever you're riding an airplane if ever the airline doesn't allow pets in the cabin as most plastic crates comply with airline safety standards.
- It's one of the most affordable crates available.
- Perhaps the only con for using a plastic crate is if you find out that your Portie doesn't prefer this type of crate since plastic crates doesn't provide vision and is quite tight.

Pros and Cons of Using Wire Crates:
- It can easily be fold up for storage or transport.
- Dogs usually like to stay in a wire crate because it provides more circulation and vision unlike with plastic crates where they're really in a tight space.
- It's also a great use while in the car if you have enough space, and it's has lots of affordable options.

- As for the cons, wire crates are quite clunky and heavy though it will depend on the size you bought.
- It's usually not allowed on planes.

Pros and Cons of Using Soft Crates:

- It's easily foldable like wire crates but the main difference is that it's made up of nylon, vinyl, and also aluminum or other lightweight materials.
- It's also best use for travels and camping.
- It's also affordable but relatively expensive than the first two types.
- The major con is that these are not recommended for dogs suffering from anxiety or those that are distressed.
- It's also not advisable for the crate training process. This is perhaps only good for dogs that have been trained already and are comfortable in using crates.

Pros and Cons of Using Fashion Crates:

- These are crates made out of finer materials that are meant to resemble furniture.

- This type of crate is best suited for dogs who have already gotten accustomed to using crates.

- It comes in various shapes and sizes

- The only con is that these crates tend to be quite expensive especially if the design is superb.

Pros and Cons of Using Heavy Duty Crates:

- These are crates that are best for long transports. It's mostly used by keepers who travel with their pets on a regular or frequent basis like those dogs who are always included in competitions or performance shows.

- This is also the safest option when travelling in cars because it's built to withstand a full on car crash.

- The only con is that these heavy duty crates are very expensive though for some it is worth the investment especially if you plan on joining competitions or travelling in different places.

Wire Crate vs. Plastic Crate

A wire crate functions as an inclusion crate, and a plastic crate is more of a quiet crate for your Portuguese water dog, both of these crates are useful for managing your pet's high energy around the house. There will be times where your dog needs to settle down and den themselves up, and there'll also be times where they need to spend time with you or your family but still needs to learn their own space, since you're there to supervise them, it's the best time to chew train your dog using chew toys, and also teach them how to use the exercise pen.

Whatever kind of crate set up you do for your pet, make sure that it's located somewhere you can adjust easily, and where you can monitor them. Don't put it in the far corner of the house or upstairs. Make it easy and convenient for both you and your pet Portie.

Here are some reminders if you will choose to use a crate:

- **It provides confinement and inclusion**: You need to somehow control your pet's stimulation and compartmentalize it in places you want. It's quite irresponsible if you just leave it up to chance, and using a crate will help.

- **It provides separation from other household pets until fully introduced and socialized.** It's best to separate your Portie once it arrives to avoid any fights and using a crate will help. Once you've properly socialize your dog with your family, you can start introducing him to your other pets but do so with precaution and make sure that you monitor their interaction.

- **It shouldn't be used for extended periods**: A crate obviously doesn't provide any outlet for your Portie's very active nature. If your dog is spending time in a crate then ensure that you counter that confinement by providing an outlet for physical exercise and mental stimulation.

- **It's not a substitute for your time and attention:** It can be an effective management tool but it's definitely not a substitute for your time and full – attention.

- **It will help your dog to adjust to its new home.** The wire crate will function as an inclusion crate wherein the dog is housed but it's still in close proximity with its owners. On the other hand, the plastic crate will function as the quiet crate which will provide your pet with some quiet time alone. Once you've crate trained your dog, you can eventually progress in housing them in the other types of crates, and they'll have no problem adjusting to it hence it will serve as their safe space.

Puppy – Proofing

First time dog owners aren't usually aware of how challenging the first few days can be especially when bringing home a young pup. If you want to avoid getting frustrated and exhausted once your new pup arrives, it's better to plan ahead of time and prepare your house for him/her.

You will need to puppy – proof your home in order to provide a hazard - free environment for your young pup. You'll need just a few hours to make your house safe once your pet arrives; puppy – proofing will set the tone for you and your pup's relationship, and will create a proper introduction to the family as well. Keep the following tips in mind:

Remove any choking hazard.

Small pieces of toys and something similar must be removed because your pup will be curious enough to swallow them. These materials can easily be swallowed by your pet and can definitely cause stomach problems. Remove any chewable items or any appliances that they can get caught up in. Secure electrical cords and anything that's hanging as well as the food in your kitchen. Once your Portie dog already demonstrated a well – behave manner, you may place the items back in the room.

Remove other potentially hazardous material out of reach.

Simple materials like matches, lighters, fire extinguishers etc. must be secured. Don't let your pup access them if you want to make sure that you still have a house to go home to. Spraying a no – chew product to the cords or other materials will make it unpleasant for the pup. Keep the puppy lock up inside its kennel if you're going to be out for a while or if you're unable to watch the puppy. Make sure to provide food, water and toys.

Remove any poisonous or harmful houseplants

Keep in mind that your Portie will almost always find something to chew on even a plant! If you have cactus inside the house, make sure it's out of reach. Check if the plants are poisonous for your pet and if so, better place them elsewhere or completely remove them.

Supplies for Your Portie

In addition to providing a crate and puppy – proofing your house, you need to also prepare the basic supplies that your Portie will need at least a few days before its scheduled arrival. You'll also need to prepare yourself because working with puppies can be quite exhausting as well.

Having the right attitude and a plan especially when it comes to feeding, exercise, grooming, training schedules and other important things will help you get things in order and save you time. The key is to enjoy the caring process, be extra patient, and just love them for who they are. Before bringing your newfound pet home, it's important that basic supplies are already prepared because this will make your pet feel safe. Make sure to ask the breeder or previous owner as to what kind of diet the puppy was raised in, if the pup has any special requirements, habits etc.

Don't forget to ask your breeder if the puppy already began training, if so, then make sure to continue the training to avoid confusion with the already established commands.

Dog crate and Exercise Pen

- It must be at least twice as large as the current size of your pup. The exercise pen can be a great integration for your dog's housetraining. It's also good for small puppies and medium - sized breeds like the Portuguese water dog. It's also a great inclusion space when your dog transition from the crate. It's very easy to set up; it's also foldable and movable plus it's quite affordable. It's important to note though that before you toss off your pet to an exercise playpen you should also spend some time training them to just play inside because if not they can easily get out once they get big enough, and it'll be useless.

Bedding Material

- It's best that you buy quality bedding that can't be easily destroyed. Make sure it's washable because it'll be prone to your pup's litter.

Puppy Collar

- Woven materials or something that's made out of soft fabric is preferred. Make sure that the collar you buy has a buckle fastener so that you can fit your puppy's neck without it being too loose or tight. A good measurement is if you can easily insert your 2 fingers between the collar and your pup's neck.

Quality lead

- This is a must especially when you take your pup out for a walk. It's highly recommended that you buy a retractable type of lead to make the dog easier to handle.

Dog Tag

- This will serve as identification if ever your puppy gets lost. Make sure to put it on their collar and include your contact details so that your puppy can be easily returned to you. This is a must even if your dog is already micro – chipped.

Grooming Supplies

- The things you'll need for grooming will depend on how wooly or fluffy your Portie's coat will be. Make sure to ask the breeder regarding what age you can start trimming your pup's coat. Usually, you need to wait until the puppy is already 10 months old. Ask your vet or breeder about it.

Chew Toys

- This is a must both for pups and even dogs. Toys will keep dog boredom at bay and it'll keep them occupied if you aren't available to play with them. The toys should preferably be plastic and doesn't become a choking hazard. If your puppy is happy with his or her toys, he or she will refrain from chewing household items or furniture.

Good quality of dog food

- Make sure to have this ready once your pup arrives. You need to ask your breeder as to what kind of diet your pup has and try to continue that by buying the same brand or offering the same amount. If you want to change their diet, make sure to do it in a gradual way so as not to upset your pup's stomach. What you can do is to combine the old diet with the new so that transition is gradual. Let your pup adjust to the new diet to prevent diarrhea.

Plastic or Stainless Food and Water Bowl

- Since pups are quite active animals, you need to make sure that you buy a food/ water bowl that can't be easily tipped over. Make sure to replenish clean water 2 times a day. Some keepers use automatic feeders but it's just optional.

Chapter Four: Food for Your Portie

Some keepers think that dog breeds are omnivores because they eat both veggies and meat which is a fact but that's only because they would pretty much eat anything. Keep in mind that canines are carnivores by nature. Their digestive system is naturally set to digest meat since they have strong and powerful digestive juices. Dogs in general are designed to eat flesh meat. If you study their anatomy, dogs have short intestines and they also have strong jaw bones, and sharp teeth that are meant to cut and rip meats. Although they can eat other type of foods like vegetables or human scrapes, their primary diet should be carnivorous.

When giving nutrition for your pet, just make sure that you never feed your pet more than the amount he/ she needs. Consult your breeder and you're your veterinarian for advice on whether your Portie needs more food or maybe additional supplements and vitamins, but do not feed him or her additional food just because he appears to be thin – looking. Most keepers switch foods once their puppy hit nine months. It's still best to consult your breeder or vet so you can ensure what age is appropriate to change their diet. Some people introduce adult food earlier than nine months, while some do it a little over ten months which is why it's best to ask your vet or breeder about it as they already have knowledge and experience regarding this matter.

The Truth About Commercial Dog Foods

Nothing comes close to feeding your Portuguese water dog or any other dog breeds for this matter with real meat. Contrary to what most people feed, real meat doesn't only pertain to muscle meat, it also includes bone and organ meat. Examples of food meals that you can feed your portie are the following:

- Chicken
- Beef
- Pork
- Turkey
- Lamb
- Fish
- Bison
- Venison
- Eggs (occasional)
- Yogurt (occasional)
- A tad of fresh veggies
- A tad of fruits

Pets deserve to eat real food meals made out of the ingredients mentioned above not just commercial dog meals such as canned dog food or dry kibbles. You can also cook for your Portie's homemade meals so that you can control what goes in your pet's diet.

According to veterinarian, Dr. Goldstein, dog and pet keepers in general can boost their pet's health by choosing to make one simple decision – to say No to commercial food and switch the diet to something of a "real food." He said that the fresh ingredients you usually purchase at the market to cook for yourself and family is the food you should also feed your pet with.

You see back then, the ancestors of many dogs lived well into their senior years and died out of old age because they only feed on fresh foods. Unfortunately, processed food came along - thanks to pet food corporations, and ruined the natural diet of the next generation of dog breeds.

Dog breeds have been domesticated for around 15,000 years already. All that time until the 1930s, these pets were given real meat, fish, and ate nothing short of fresh ingredients. They all thrived on this kind of diet and most of them lived into their old age.

1930s was when the meat and grain industry started to market their rejected ingredients to animals. The ingredients weren't able to pass the USDA inspection because the wheat and corn content is not safe for people due to contaminants, mold, and rancidity. And because of this, the manufacturers need to find a way to make a return of investment and at the same time dispose their stocks of rejected ingredients. This is how "pet food" was born.

Pet food is the manufacturers' idea of mixing rejected ingredients and packaging them in a way that it's a commercial processed food for pets. With the help of advertisements and marketing firms, the idea was planted in the public's mind. Until today, commercial diets are being aggressively advertised by huge pet food corporations including the veterinary industry since they both have large financial stake in this business idea.

Many owners are now realizing that processed dry kibbles and canned products were never the kind of food that any pet is born to eat. And thanks to the internet, more and more keepers are becoming aware of this truth and they are switching their dog's diet back to an all – natural diet.

Another veterinarian named Dr. Pitcairn said that dogs eating kibbles or commercial foods their whole life is similar to humans eating nothing but fast foods like burgers and fries. At some point, you would be desperate to eat something fresh like a salad or fruit. This is human nature, we're all designed to eat something whole and raw, and it is very similar to pets in general. All living creatures need to have unprocessed and wholesome food included in our daily diet.

Harmful Ingredients in Commercial Dog Foods

To give you an idea of how commercial dog foods can affect your Portie's health and lifestyle in the long run, you must know the implications of the ingredients contained in each bag of commercial and processed dog food. The aim of this section is to show you just how harmful feeding nothing but commercial foods to your dogs can ultimately take a toll on them. Hopefully, you'll switch to more fresh and natural ingredients.

Grain

Almost all commercial dog foods consist of cereals and fiber – heavy grains. What you need to know is that dogs don't have a long digestive tract which means that they can't easily digest fiber – heavy grains unlike us humans. Their short digestive tract is only built to digest meat.

Over the years, dog breeds that consume wheat, corn and soybean products eventually develop various health issues such as itchy skin, loose feces, excessive dandruff and shedding, flatulence and gassiness. Most owners don't have any idea that all these health problems are usually connected to the ingredients they fed on their pet's diet.

Meat

The only time that you should consider buying a dog food brand is when it has a guarantee from the USDA inspection. Unless it says "Passed," it didn't. What most dog food brands advertise is that your dog gets sirloin from a cow raised in lush pasture but nothing could be further from the truth. Same with chickens, your dog doesn't get healthy chicken meat from hens that happily pecked in the barnyard, and this is because usually meat from chickens and cows are jammed together in warehouses where these animals are treated inhumanely. This is the reason why the meat fails to pass the standard of the human market because it usually has 4D characteristics – Diseased, Disabled, Dying or Dead. In addition, these kinds of 4D meats also contain growth hormones and antibiotics when the livestock were still alive to prevent massive disease outbreaks and make them grow faster. However, such growth hormones and antibiotics trickle down to your pet causing health issues in the long – term.

Greasy Fat

Greasy fat is the pungent smell when you open up a bag of dry kibble. It's usually sprayed into the pebbles so that your dog will become enticed in eating it. If manufacturers didn't do that, your dog will not recognize the dry kibble as food. It's quite similar to kids eating French Fries - the smell of fried potatoes attract kids (and adults), but parents don't just let their kids eat junk food right? It should be the same with dogs.

Preservatives

Just like in any other type of foods, preservatives can make food ingredients last for a long time. This is of course beneficial to the commercial dog food manufacturers since it can stay in their storage for quite some time. It's also beneficial for retailers and even keepers because it can stay on the shelf or pantry for a period of time. However, it's not convenient for your dog's health.

You see, preservatives in pet foods include BHT and BHA which according to the World Health Organization is the probable cause of cancer – not just in pets but also in humans.

Another chemical that preservatives have is called ethoxyquin which is a rubber preservative, and classified by the Department of Agriculture as a pesticide, while OSHA deems it as a hazardous and poisonous chemical. Come to think of it, these harmful chemicals will eventually trickle down to your pet Portie.

Keep in mind that even if those preservatives are not listed in the dog food package, it might still be contaminated with it. This is because multi – billion dollar dog food companies can create legal loopholes so that they can only list ingredients that they want the customers to see. Needless to say, if the dog food manufacturer purchases ingredients from a supplier who already added such preservative chemicals, the manufacturer doesn't need to necessarily disclose that information which means consumers are being fooled.

Filler Ingredients

How about the unknown ingredients? Some of these things include beet pulp, wheat bran, corn gluten, and brewer's rice to name a few. Most consumers have no idea what these ingredients are but because it sounds nutritional most dog keepers buy food brands containing such "filler" ingredients. According to Animal Digest, these ingredients are materials that resulted from chemical hydrolysis of un-decomposed animal tissue.

Filler ingredients are usually a boiled concoction of animal tissues which can include roadkill and dead pets as well as rats or other animals euthanized at the animal shelter. It sounds so gross I know, but imagine if this is the kind of stuff that your dog is eating, no wonder why most of them die at a young age. The Food and Drug Administration has found pentobarbital chemical in some dog food brands. The pentobarbital chemical is what's being used to euthanize animals. Yikes!

According to Australian vet, Dr. Billinghurst, most of the ingredients listed of a bag of pet food are rubbish. This is because if you truly look into it, it's not the kind of wholesome nutritious meal you would want to give to a valued member of your family. That's how awful most commercial dog brands are. We hope you get to see the point of why it's very important to feed your dogs with fresh and wholesome meals instead of dog foods made out of nothing but gross preservatives.

How dog food affects your dog's health

These are some of the most common illnesses that dogs suffer from due to eating commercial dog foods:

- Coat and skin problems

- Digestive tract issues
- Joint Problems

The most common denominator of dogs suffering from such illnesses is that they are all being fed with either a canned food or dry kibbles all their lives.

Homemade Meals for Your Portie

The easiest way to feed your Portuguese water dog with homemade diet if you haven't got the time to do all that is to just buy it from the store. There are food brands that have a mixture of fruits, veggies, and minced meat all together. It's frozen and ready to go whenever you need to feed your dog. You can also crack an egg to top it off, and provide a raw chicken with bone. Make sure that the chicken bone is raw; otherwise the bones will splinter and could get stuck in your dog's digestive track. Raw chicken bones are chewy and great for your pet Portie. Aside from raw chicken bones, you can add beef chunks on its meal. It's up to you on what other veggies, fruits or meat you want to add but just make sure that you've consulted your vet regarding the ingredients you're going to add to ensure that it would be healthy for your pet

Once you have decided on what kind of food you're going to feed your Portie, the next step is to decide how you're going to feed them. Most keepers schedule their dog's feeding. Scheduled feeding is when the food of your Portie is offered for up to 15 to 20 minutes only before removing it whether it's eaten by your pet or not. This is quite an effective habit especially for indoor pets because it also helps you out when planning for their walks, play time, and exercise breaks.

On the other hand, free feeding is when you simply place an automatic feeder or offer your pet with a bowl of food that they can access whenever they want. Free feeding is usually the culprit to obesity because the dog can eat anytime he wants. Free feeding may not be a good idea if you have other pets or dogs inside the house because they could steal food from one another. The dominant dog usually has the authority to eat the food of the submissive dogs. This could start conflicts and aggression towards your pets. If you choose free feeding, make sure that their food bowls are placed in their own crates and the other pets won't have any access to it other than their own feeders.

Chapter Five: Crate Training and Grooming

One of the major cons of owning a Portuguese water dog aside from keeping up with its active lifestyle is its coat maintenance or the grooming part, and that's mainly because even if these dogs aren't shedders, their coats are sometimes quite hard to trim and brush especially if you decided to do it yourself, and not bring him to a local groomer. You should also keep in mind to never shave your Portie's coat. A dog's coat protects them from varying environmental conditions. If you want your pet to maintain a nice soft or silky fur, you can do that by feeding them with foods like fish that are rich with omega fatty acids.

These types of food can help improve your pet's skin, make their coat glossy, and maintain their hypoallergenic characteristic.

When it comes to crate training, never force your pet to live in it if they don't feel comfortable inside because it may worsen their distress in the long run. Keep in mind that your goal here is to let your dog view the crate as a safe place that's also a pleasant and comfortable environment. This is why habituating them is important. Your goal is to have a good conditional emotional response from your Portie. If ever your pet had a previous bad experience when it comes to being housed in crates or he or she is suffering from separation anxiety or isolation distress, then you may need to ask help from a professional dog trainer or behavioral consultant. This chapter will guide you on how you can properly crate train and groom your Portie.

Brushing Your Portie

Step #1: Get a shed blade and brush off the clumps of hair of your Portie.

Get rid of the clumps of hair using a shed blade. Brush your Portie with a coat rake or other brush that would best suit your Portie's coat. You can start from the head and work towards the rest of its body.

Step #2: Loosen up your Portie's coat by using water and conditioner. The conditioner will help control the loosen furs and also prevent hurting as you untangle some mats in your pet's coat.

Step #3: Use the comb to untangle the mats and knots if there's any and loosen the dead hair. Don't pull off the mats as this will hurt your pet. Brush the coat all over its body by using a fine – toothed comb to also brush the fur under its skin, chin, tail, and ears. Take the brush and comb its coat forward over its head and shoulders. Remember to also comb out the hair in its legs and rear end. Use the metal comb to brush the coat and flatten it out, then add some finishing touches by using a regular pin brush. You can also trim up some excess fur in its feet or toes to make him look neat.

Basic Training for Your Pup

As with any other dog training, timing is everything. You need to be able to monitor your pet's energy. Never try to crate train them during their peak arousal times or a period within the day where you think they are most active. Ideally, you want to crate train them once they've already worn out or tired after playing around all day because that will initiate them to settle down inside their crate and take some rest after a long day. Here are some tips for properly crate training your portie pup:

Keep in mind that your voice is first and foremost your training tool. You need to also consider using a consistent phrase to cue your pet to go inside its crate. Pairing a word or phrase will help when you're instructing your pet and catching their attention towards where it needs to be.

Keep them safe and secure inside. You should initially use a lock or something so that the door wouldn't swing back and forth so that it wouldn't scare your Portie.

Use a bowl of treats as a pre – bait for your portie during training. Keeping a bowl of treats when you're doing crate training will be handy because it will function as pre – bait for your dog. Chew toys is also essential because you'll need to reward it afterwards. Never crate train your dog if you don't have food and toy rewards. You must set it up beforehand so that it can be convenient for you once you start training your pet.

Prepare 'unpredictable routines'. Routines are great but make sure that your training follow – up is not predictable for your pet. What you need to do is to destabilize any pattern that will short – circuit your dog's expectation. This way it will help preserve the integrity of your crate training. Keep in mind that Porties are very clever dogs, and if they can predict the activities you've prepared for them, they might easily get bored by it overtime. Make sure to rotate training activities.

Practice your portie to voluntarily go to the crate. As you may now know, crate training is quite labor intensive but it lessens the onset of many problems in the long run. You need to be patient and continue practicing your pet to go to the crate willingly. It may probably take several days to a few weeks or maybe even longer so don't rush it.

Chapter Six: Purebred Standards and Showing Your Portie

You might be convinced that you want a purebred dog like the Portuguese water dog but often times, people who choose purebred dogs are only basing their decisions on the pros without considering the cons. The decision of getting a purebred dog over a mixed breed or a crossbreed should be after you hear both the positives and negatives. There are lots of books and online resources out there that only discuss the positives but leave out the negatives. This chapter will provide you with a more balanced perspective about purebred dogs so that you'll know the truth about their characteristics and traits as well as the advantage and disadvantages of keeping one so that you can make a wise and informed decision.

We will also provide you with the official breed standard of the Portuguese Water Dog breed from the American Kennel Club (AKC) which can come in handy if you would eventually want to sign up your pet portie for a show or for various dog competitions.

Pros of Owning Purebred Dogs

You can easily predict the physical traits of a purebred canine.

Puppies grow up and look a lot like their parents despite each of them having their own unique set of genes. Just like in humans, the genes produce the desired traits for a particular breed – in this case a Portuguese water dog. The desired traits usually include the color, coat, erect ears or not, size of the breed etc.

The breeders are the one who ultimately decides which traits are desirable, and they will try to produce those traits as they further develop a particular breed. When breeds with the wanted characteristics are developed, the genes that have such traits will spread throughout the gene pool of that particular breed.

For instance, when you see a puppy that's a member of a certain breed, you'll have an idea which genes or desired traits were inherited. If you prefer to acquire a certain length of coat, or dog size, you can choose a breed that carries the genes of such traits. For many people, the appearance is the most predictable trait of purebred dogs.

You can predict some of the behavioral traits of a purebred canine.

Genes also carry some aspects of behavior and personality. For instance, Portuguese water dogs are known for their high energy; this means that the Portie breed inherited genes with high energy. You can choose dog breeds that carry genes with your desired personality/ behavioral traits such as dog breeds that are known for herding cattles, watchdog, rodent hunters, or in the Portie breed's case someone that is hardworking and a water – loving dog. You can choose a dog breed that tends to inherit such kinds of temperament. However, keep in mind that some behavioral and personality aspects are not inherited, instead it is more based on the dog's environment – how they are raised and trained since they were young. There are some dogs that are more affected by their genes while there are some that are more affected by how they were raised.

Another thing you need to keep in mind when it comes to behavioral traits is that these are already hardwired in your dog's genes which mean that it can be hard to change. Therefore, in order to minimize stress and struggles on your part, you should look for a breed or a puppy that already possess a temperament you prefer or something that you can handle.

Cons of Owning Purebred Dogs

Predictable Physical Characteristics means that you're stuck with it.

There are many newbie dog keepers that acquire a purebred dog and then complain later on about its "built – in" traits. This is why it's very important that whenever you choose a certain breed as pet, you need to make sure that you can handle its physical traits and characteristics. Consider the following questions relating to physical characteristics:

- How much does this dog breed shed?
- How much brushing do they need in a day or week?
- How much exercise or daily activities do they require?
- If they're small, can I keep them safe? If they're large, can I provide an adequate shelter or space?

Many purebred dogs have working traits that can sometimes be difficult to live with.

As with Portuguese water dogs, you'll most likely have a problem with their chewing and the need to do something since they are used to working hard for fishermen back in the day. Other breeds are somewhat the same; they are developed to do some type of work like hunting rodents or rabbits, herding cattle, guarding the livestock, pulling sleds or carts, doing military/ police work and the likes. So if you just want to have a family companion or a lap dog, purebred canine is definitely not for you. Their working traits can be a nuisance for you so make sure to consider that aspect.

Some behavioral traits that helped a purebred canine do its work include the following:
- High energy level – it can be hard to keep up with them and they can get bored easily if you don't prepare any activities or spend time with them.

- Independent – it can be hard for them to follow what you want because they are clever and have a mind of their own.
- Strong desire to do "work" – if they don't find anything worth it to do, they might end up digging in your backyard or ruining your furniture.
- Chasing and nipping – they might always chase other household pets or even gnaw at your hands.
- Aggression toward other dog breeds – it can be due to their protective instincts.
- Suspiciousness toward strangers
- Howling or barking

Many purebred dogs don't guarantee that they act or look the way you expect.

A purebred pup can grow up to act or look differently that what you expected. The predictability factors that we've discussed earlier are typical but not always guaranteed. Just like humans, there are some purebred canines that do not "conform to the status quo" of their breed.

Purebred dogs are prone to many health issues.

Here are some of the health issues that most purebred

canines develop over time:

- Joint Disorders – this can cause mobility issues and crippling bones
- Eye Diseases – it can range from reduced eyesight to total blindness
- Heart Diseases – it can ultimately shorten a dog's life and create other complications
- Endocrine System Diseases – it can cause major illnesses like diabetes and hypothyroidism
- Seizure Disorders – includes epilepsy and other neurological related illnesses
- Digestive Tract Disorders – includes flatulence, diarrhea, vomiting, and gassiness.
- Kidney and Liver Diseases, Blood – clotting Diseases and Cancer these are the major diseases that kills many dog breeds.

There are 300 genetic health issues that occur in dogs but it's not just limited to purebred canines; it also includes mixed and crossbreeds though the risk of these health problems usually occur more in purebred canines than in mixed breeds or crossbreeds.

A purebred dog may be right for you if…

- If you know the characteristics and traits you want in a breed
- If there is a dog breed that has all or at least most of the traits you're looking for and that it's something you can handle.
- If you will gladly accept the other undesirable traits that the breed may have
- If you're willing to accept the risk of health issues
- If you are willing to pay a certain amount to acquire a puppy from a reputable source, or have the time to adopt a dog from a rescue shelter.
- If you are willing to acquire a puppy from someone who you know produces healthy and good – tempered purebred canine.

Portuguese Water Dog Official Breed Standard

General Appearance:

- Robust and medium – sized dog
- Spirited yet naturally obedient
- Developed for a full day's work both in and out of the water
- An excellent diver and swimmer
- Has exceptional stamina and ability
- Known for retrieving nets, carrying messages, and herding fishes
- A loyal breed and an excellent watch dog
- A very energetic, independent and highly intelligent dog
- Sports either a wavy or curly coat
- Has an impressive head structure
- The mass is well – proportioned
- Have a well – knit body structure and a thick based tail
- Can gallantly carry himself and has great stride
- Leaves an impression of spirit, soundness and strength

Size and Weight:

- The height for male Portuguese water dog breeds should be between 20 and 23 inches. 22 inches is preferred.

- The height for female Portuguese water dog breeds should be between 17 and 21 inches. 19 inches is preferred.

- The weight for males should be between 42 and 60 pounds while females should be between 35 and 50 pounds

Proportion and Substance:

- The proportion must be off – square which means that the breed must slightly be longer than tall if measured from the prosternum to the rearmost point of the butt as well as from the withers to the ground.

- The substance of the breed must be strong, well developed and has a substantial bone that is neither coarse nor refined. The body must be muscular and has a solid built.

Head:

- The head must be well – proportioned and large but it should have an exceptional breadth in the top skull.

- The expression of the breed should preferably be steady, attentive and penetrating.

- The eyes should be set well apart, medium in size and a bit oblique. It should roundish and not sunken or prominent. Darker colors of eyes are preferred but other eye colors such as black and varying shade of brown is also acceptable. The eye rims should be fully pigmented with black edges in black, black and white or white Porties, and brown edges in brown Porties. The haws must be dark in color and not apparent.

- The ears must be set well above the line of the Portie's eye. The leather must be thin and heart – shape. The ears must be held against the head except for the small opening at the back. Tips shouldn't reach below the dog's lower jaw.

- The skull must be slightly longer than the dog's muzzle. The breed's curvature should be more prominent at the back than in its front. If viewed from the top, the top of the skull should appear domed and broad with a slight depression in the center. The forehead should be prominent and it must have a middle furrow that extends to about 2/3 of the distance from stop to occiput. The occiput and stop must both be well – defined.

- The muzzle should be substantial and preferably wider at the base than at the breed's nose.

- The jaw should neither be overshot nor undershot and it must be strong.

- The nose should possess a well – flared nostrils and preferably broad. It should also be fully – pigmented; it should have black pigmentation for Porties that sport a black, black and white, or white coats. For porties sporting brown coats, the nose pigmentation can have varying degree of brown shade.

- Lips should be thick particularly in the front and must have no flew. The mucous membrane under the tongue, on the gums and at the roof of its mouth should be blackish in color or well – ticked in Porties that sport a black, black and white, or white coats; porties that sport a brown color must have varying tones of brown.

- The bite must be level or scissors
- The teeth must be visible when mouth is closed

Neck, Topline, and Body:

- The neck must be strongly muscled. It should be round, short, held high and straight with no dewlap.
- The topline should be firm and leveled.
- The chest should be reaching down to the dog's elbow. It must be deep and broad
- The ribs must be well – sprung and long so that it can provide the optimum lung capacity for the portie.
- The abdomen must be held up with grace. The back should be well – muscled and broad. The croup must be well – formed and should only be slightly inclined with the dog's hip bones. The loin should also meet the croup smoothly and it must be short.
- The tail should be thick at the base and not docked. It must also be tapering and shouldn't reach below the

dog's hock. The tail preferably should be slightly below the line of the dog's back. When the Portie is attentive, the tail must be held in a ring. And the front should not reach forward of the breed's loin. The tail is beneficial whenever the dog is diving and swimming.

Forequarters

- Shoulders of the breed should be strongly muscled and well – inclined. The upper arms must be strong.
- The forelegs of the breed should be strong, straight and well – muscled.
- The carpus should be heavy – boned and must be wider in the front than on the side.
- Pasterns should be strong and long.
- Dewclaws must be removed and the feet should not be flat but round.
- The toes should not be too long or knuckled up.
- Webbing between the dog's toes should be well – covered with hair and a soft skin. It should also reach the toe tips.

- Central pad should be quite thick and but other pads should be normal.
- Nails must be slightly held up off the ground
- Striped, black, white and brown nails are acceptable.

Hindquarters:

- Hindlegs must be well – balanced with the front assembly and should be powerful.
- When viewed from the rear, the legs should be parallel to each other and must be strong and straight particularly in the lower and upper thighs. The butt must be well – developed.
- The tendons and hocks should be strong
- The metatarsus must have no dewclaws and it should be long
- The feet must be similar in all respects

Coat:

- The coat should be profuse, thick and must cover the entire body evenly. It must consists of health hair, and there should be thin hair where the forearm meets the groin and brisket area

- Portuguese water dogs have no undercoat, ruff or mane.
- There are 2 types of coat that Porties sport these are:
- Curly Coat: Must be lusterless, compact and compose of cylindrical curls. The hair on the ears can be a bit wavy.
- Wavy Coat: Must have no curls, and should fall gently in the waves with a slight sheen.

Clip:

There are 2 acceptable clips for Portuguese water dogs:

- o Lion Clip: As soon as the coat of the Porties grows long, the muzzle, hindquarters and middle part should be clipped. The hair at the end of its tail should be at full length.

- o Retriever Clip: The entire coat of the portie should be clipped or scissored so that it will have a natural appearance and so that it will follow the outline of the breed. The smooth unbroken like should leave a short blanket of coat that's no longer than 1 inch in length. The hair at the end of its tail should also be at full length.

Color:

- Porties can sport the following coat colors: black, brown, white as well as black and white or brown with white.
- Having a white coat doesn't imply albinism as long as the mouth, eyelids, and nose are black in color.
- For porties that sport a white, black, or black and white coats, the skin is usually bluish

Gait:

- The portie must have lively and forward stride
- It must be short and well – balanced

Temperament:

- The Portuguese water dog is resistant to fatigue, has a spirited disposition, and self – willed/ independent.

- It's one of the most exceptionally intelligent dog breed and knows how to obey its owner with apparent pleasure.
- He is a loyal and compassionate companion who looks after his owners.

Faults:

- Any deviation from the described standards aforementioned
- The inherent traits that are imperative for proper maintenance shouldn't be overlooked otherwise it will be concluded as Major Faults

Major Faults

- Temperament: If the Portie is vicious, has an unsound behavior or shy
- Head: If the topskull is narrow, if it has a snipey muzzle, if the head is small in size and unimpressive
- Substance: If the bone is refined and light or if it lacks in muscle

- Coat: If it is naturally short, close – lying, brittle, wispy in texture or double – coated.

- Tail: If the tail is heavy, droopy or has extremely low set.

- Pigment: Any deviation from the standard mentioned above. If the nose, eye rims, eyes, or lips are pink or has partial pigmentation.

- Bite: If it is undershot or overshot

Chapter Seven: Health Information for Porties

All dog breeds have the possibility of developing genetic health issues just as all humans have the possibility of inheriting a particular disease from their parents or family lineage. That being said, it's highly recommended that you only purchase a Portuguese water dog breed from a reputable source who offers a health guarantee on the pups they sell. If a breeder tells you that the litter he/ she is selling is 100% healthy or has no known health issue, our advice to you is run, don't walk! If the breeder is a reputable one he/ she will be open and honest about any health problems in the dog, or the incidences with which such issues occur in the breed's lineage.

Most portie breeds are at risk of developing hip dysplasia which is a disorder of the hip socket that can make your pet suffer from mobility issues and become crippled overtime especially if not prevented. This health issue usually needs surgery treatment. However, even if hip dysplasia is corrected, most dogs eventually get stricken with arthritis as they grow older.

Portuguese water dog breed can also develop different genetic eye abnormalities. One of which is called microphthalmia. This is often diagnosed through an eye exam. Some breeders haven't got their litter go through an eye exam which is why it's prudent that you do so in order for your dog to prevent further eye problems in the future. The results should also be filed to the Canine Eye Registration Foundation (CERF), though it is optional.

In addition to microphthalmia, another eye problem that affects most Porties is a disease known as Progressive Retinal Atrophy (PRA). You can have your pup or adult dog go through a genetic screening test to ensure that your Portie is free from such disease. The breeder whom you acquired your Portie from should show you a genetic screening test of the puppy's parent breed as well. You can have such genetic test through Optigen or for more information, go to the website of the Portuguese Water Dog Club of America (PWDCA) at www.pwdca.org

Another health issue that usually affects Porties is called the GM1 gangliosidosis. This is the kind of disease that is fatal not just for the Portie breed but also for other dog breeds. It's usually caused by the toxin build – up in the nerve cells of a dog/ puppy. Thanks to the determined efforts of the PWDCA, DNA testing was developed and for several years pups haven't been affected by this rare and potentially fatal illness. You should never acquire a pup from a source that can't provide you with a written documentation of the GM1 gangliosidosis status of the pup's parents.

Other diseases that may affect the Portie canine include but are not limited to the following:

- Heart – Related Problems
- Thyroid Problems
- Sebaceous Adenitis (this is caused by the inflammation of the dog's sebaceous glands which can lead to skin diseases and hair loss.

The PWDCA highly recommend that keepers and would – be Portie owners conduct a genetic screening for the diseases/ health problems mentioned above. Your puppy source should also be eager and willing to explain to you the health histories of the pup's parents as well as their family lineage. He/ she must discuss how prevalent health concerns are in the pup's dog's family line.

The Portuguese Water Dog Club of America is a member of the health database in the United States known as the Canine Health Information Center (CHIC). For a Portuguese Water Dog to become CHIC certified, the breeder should get a hip evaluation, an eye clearance, DNA test results, and GM1 gangliosidosis DNA test to the

Orthopedic Foundation for Animals (OFA), the CERF, PRA,

and OFA again respectively. Yearly eye examinations are

recommended until the canine reaches 10 years old.

Other optional tests include the following:

- Cardiac evaluation

- Sebaceous adenitis evaluation

- Thyroid evaluation

- Juvenile dilated cardiomyopathy evaluation

The breeder that you're going to acquire from must agree

to publish all the test results (both positive and negative) in

the CHIC database. A dog breed don't need to have passing

scores on the various evaluations for him to get a CHIC

number. CHIC registration is not proof that a dog has no

disease but all test results are posted on the website of CHIC

which can be accessed by anyone who may want to check

the health of the pup's parents.

In addition to all of these, perhaps the most common and deadly health issue that most dogs face is none other than obesity. This is pretty much the responsibility of the owner – you, to ensure that your Portie pup gets the right nutrition and adequate exercise so that you can easily extend their life and keep them healthy. As with humans, prevention is always better than cure. It's up to you on how you can help your Portuguese water dog live a healthy, happy and long life.

Pet Insurance for Dogs

What is Pet Insurance and how does it work?

Pet insurance is similar to getting your own health insurance. Your Portie pet basically gets treatment if he/she acquires any illness or experienced some sort of accident. Needless to say, the insurance company pays most of the vet bills. Unfortunately, family health insurance doesn't cover household pets even if we can all argue that they are all "part of the family." This is why pets have their own policy that can protect them should the need arise.

If ever your dog got into an accident or acquired an illness, you can take him/ her to the vet or a specialist. And just like health policies for humans, you just send the copies of the vet's bills to the pet insurance company. The company will pay for your dog's treatment but the coverage will depend on the terms of your chosen policy.

Usually, pet insurance companies pay around 70 to 90% of the bills and the rest is paid by the owner; this known as co – pay. There is also a deductible wherein the owner shoulders the payments temporarily before the insurance payment and co – pay are calculated. If you have chosen a higher deductible/ co – pay that means your monthly premium is less. Some owners choose to have a lower co – pay/ deductible and they let the company pay more for the final bill. This is up to you to choose the best policy for you and your Portie water dog.

Why do my dog needs a pet insurance?

It is for the same reason why you get a health insurance or a family health coverage – for the purpose of lessening the financial burden if in case an accident happens or an illness occur. Similar to health policies for you or your family, it's up to you if you want to be insured or not. Obviously if you don't, you'll have to pay all the medical bills yourself.

If you are well enough to carry the bills without straining your budget, or compromising the treatment that you pet receives, then most probably your dog doesn't need insurance. On the other hand, if you are not rich enough to pay for your dog's medical bills or you only have a budget every month, it would be wise to pay a monthly premium in exchange for the financial as well as emotional security of knowing that your portie will be able to get medical treatment that he/she may need without breaking the bank.

In addition to all of these, keep in mind that all canines have genetic weaknesses and most breeds no matter how healthy they are, are still susceptible to various illnesses such as cancer, epilepsy, heart problems, hip dysplasia, kidney and liver diseases, respiratory illnesses etc. Modern diagnostic tests and treatments are now available for dogs but they are very expensive. Knee replacements, allergy testing, chiropractic care and invasive cancer surgeries are some of the advance treatments available as of this writing.

How much vet medications and treatments cost?

Health care for humans are becoming more and more expensive as the technology gets more advanced than ever. The increasing diagnostics and treatment rates happening in the health care industry are also happening in vet medicine. This is because such treatments and tests that were originally developed for humans are now being used for pets. Below are some examples of treatments and tests that pet insurance company pay for along with their costs.

Condition: Limping

Advanced Diagnostics/ Treatments:

- Digital X-Ray
- CT Scan
- MRI
- Laser Therapy
- Chiropractic Care
- Acupuncture
- Massage Therapy

Cost: $5,000

Condition: Digestive Issues

Advanced Diagnostics/ Treatments:

- Digital X-Ray
- Endoscopy
- Ultrasound
- CT scan
- Intestinal Biopsy

Cost: $6,400

Condition: Growth or Lump

Advanced Diagnostics/ Treatments:

- Biopsies
- Radiation
- Chemotherapy
- Cyberknife

Cost: $15,000

Condition: Heart – Related Conditions

Advanced Diagnostics/ Treatments: Major surgeries &
follow up treatments

Cost: $20,000

What are the things covered by pet insurance?

You may want to get a policy that covers the following conditions:

- Common illnesses and chronic conditions
- Injuries and accidents
- Congenital and hereditary Conditions
- Cancer
- X – Rays
- Diagnostic and blood tests
- CT Scans/ MRI
- Ultrasounds
- Surgery and hospitalization
- Emergency and specialty care
- Prescription medications and alternative treatments

No pet insurance company covers what they call as pre – existing conditions. This means it is suicide for pet insurance companies – financially speaking to let every pet owner sign up for their insurance policy before keepers get expensive treatments for their pets.

Pet insurance policy covers any vet, animal clinic, specialists or hospitals as well as treatments. The most important thing to cover are genetic and hereditary conditions since these are among the most expensive health issues to treat. You can also opt to cover alternative treatments such as cold laser therapy, acupuncture, and hydrotherapy.

What's not covered by pet insurance?

In addition to pre – existing conditions, most pet insurance companies don't cover routine vaccinations, dental cleaning, yearly checkups, exam fees, and non – emergency neutering.

Glossary of Dog Terms

Abundism – Referring to a pup that has markings more prolific than is normal.

Acariasis – A type of mite infection.

ACF – Australian Pup Federation

Affix – A puptery name that follows the pup's registered name; puptery owner, not the breeder of the pup.

Agouti – A type of natural coloring pattern in which individual hairs have bands of light and dark coloring.

Ailurophile – A person who loves pups.

Albino – A type of genetic mutation which results in little to no pigmentation, in the eyes, skin, and coat.

Allbreed – Referring to a show that accepts all breeds or a judge who is qualified to judge all breeds.

Alley Pup – A non-pedigreed pup.

Alter – A desexed pup; a male pup that has been neutered or a female that has been spayed.

Amino Acid – The building blocks of protein; there are 22 types for pups, 11 of which can be synthesized and 11 which must come from the diet (see essential amino acid).

Anestrus – The period between estrus cycles in a female pup.

Any Other Variety (AOV) – A registered pup that doesn't conform to the breed standard.

ASH – American Shorthair, a breed of pup.

Back Cross – A type of breeding in which the offspring is mated back to the parent.

Balance – Referring to the pup's structure; proportional in accordance with the breed standard.

Barring – Describing the tabby's striped markings.

Base Color – The color of the coat.

Bicolor – A pup with patched color and white.

Blaze – A white coloring on the face, usually in the shape of an inverted V.

Bloodline – The pedigree of the pup.

Brindle – A type of coloring, a brownish or tawny coat with streaks of another color.

Castration – The surgical removal of a male pup's testicles.

Pup Show – An event where pups are shown and judged.

Puptery – A registered pup breeder; also, a place where pups may be boarded.

CFA – The Pup Fanciers Association.

Cobby – A compact body type.

Colony – A group of pups living wild outside.

Color Point – A type of coat pattern that is controlled by color point alleles; pigmentation on the tail, legs, face, and ears with an ivory or white coat.

Colostrum – The first milk produced by a lactating female; contains vital nutrients and antibodies.

Conformation – The degree to which a pedigreed pup adheres to the breed standard.

Cross Breed – The offspring produced by mating two distinct breeds.

Dam – The female parent.

Declawing – The surgical removal of the pup's claw and first toe joint.

Developed Breed – A breed that was developed through selective breeding and crossing with established breeds.

Down Hairs – The short, fine hairs closest to the body which keep the pup warm.

DSH – Domestic Shorthair.

Estrus – The reproductive cycle in female pups during which she becomes fertile and receptive to mating.

Fading Pup Syndrome – Pups that die within the first two weeks after birth; the cause is generally unknown.

Feral – A wild, untamed pup of domestic descent.

Gestation – Pregnancy; the period during which the fetuses develop in the female's uterus.

Guard Hairs – Coarse, outer hairs on the coat.

Harlequin – A type of coloring in which there are van markings of any color with the addition of small patches of the same color on the legs and body.

Inbreeding – The breeding of related pups within a closed group or breed.

Kibble – Another name for dry pup food.

Lilac – A type of coat color that is pale pinkish-gray.

Line – The pedigree of ancestors; family tree.

Litter – The name given to a group of pups born at the same time from a single female.

Mask – A type of coloring seen on the face in some breeds.

Matts – Knots or tangles in the pup's fur.

Mittens – White markings on the feet of a pup.

Moggie – Another name for a mixed breed pup.

Mutation – A change in the DNA of a cell.

Muzzle – The nose and jaws of an animal.

Natural Breed – A breed that developed without selective breeding or the assistance of humans.

Neutering – Desexing a male pup.

Open Show – A show in which spectators are allowed to view the judging.

Pads – The thick skin on the bottom of the feet.

Particolor – A type of coloration in which there are markings of two or more distinct colors.

Patched – A type of coloration in which there is any solid color, tabby, or tortoiseshell color plus white.

Pedigree – A purebred pup; the pup's papers showing its family history.

Pet Quality – A pup that is not deemed of high enough standard to be shown or bred.

Piebald – A pup with white patches of fur.

Points – Also color points; markings of contrasting color on the face, ears, legs, and tail.

Pricked – Referring to ears that sit upright.

Purebred – A pedigreed pup.

Queen – An intact female pup.

Roman Nose – A type of nose shape with a bump or arch.

Scruff – The loose skin on the back of a pup's neck.

Selective Breeding – A method of modifying or improving a breed by choosing pups with desirable traits.

Senior – A pup that is more than 5 but less than 7 years old.

Sire – The male parent of a pup.

Solid – Also self; a pup with a single coat color.

Spay – Desexing a female pup.

Stud – An intact male pup.

Tabby – A type of coat pattern consisting of a contrasting color over a ground color.

Tom Pup – An intact male pup.

Tortoiseshell – A type of coat pattern consisting of a mosaic of red or cream and another base color.

Tri-Color – A type of coat pattern consisting of three distinct colors in the coat.

Tuxedo – A black and white pup.

Unaltered – A pup that has not been desexed

Photo Credits

References

Dog Health Care & Feeding – The Sensible Way - YourPureBredPuppy.com

https://www.yourpurebredpuppy.com/health/articles/dog-health-care-intro.html

Portuguese Water Dog: A Guide for Breeders - PWDCA.org

https://www.pwdca.org/assets/docs/library/pwdca_breeder_guide_201108.pdf

Portuguese Water Dogs in Canada - PWDCC.org

http://pwdcc.org/wp-content/uploads/2017/11/pwdcc-handout-brochure.pdf

Portuguese Water Dogs - FCI.be

http://www.fci.be/Nomenclature/Standards/037g08-en.pdf

Portuguese Water Dog - CKC.ca

https://www.ckc.ca/CanadianKennelClub/media/Breed-Standards/Group%203/Portuguese-Water-Dog.pdf

Portuguese Water Dog - Temperament & Personality - Petwave.com

https://www.petwave.com/Dogs/Breeds/Portuguese-Water-Dog/Personality.aspx

Portuguese Water Dog - Vetstreet.com

http://www.vetstreet.com/dogs/portuguese-water-dog

Feeding the Portuguese Water Dog - RawLearning.com

http://www.rawlearning.com/rawpwd.pdf

Frequently Asked Questions About Portuguese Water Dogs - YourPureBredPuppy.com

https://www.yourpurebredpuppy.com/faq/portuguesewater dogs.html

The Truth About Mixed Breed Dogs - YourPureBredPuppy.com

https://www.yourpurebredpuppy.com/buying/articles/mixe d-breed-dogs.html

Vaccinations and Booster Shots: Needed or Not? - YourPureBredPuppy.com

https://www.yourpurebredpuppy.com/health/articles/pupp y-shots-and-dog-vaccinations.html

Pet Insurance Review – Should You Buy Pet Insurance? - YourPureBredPuppy.com

https://www.yourpurebredpuppy.com/health/articles/pet-insurance.html

www.ingramcontent.com/pod-product-compliance
Lightning Source LLC
Chambersburg PA
CBHW061958040426
42447CB00010B/1805